Understanding Your Income Taxes

SOUTH-WESTERN

UNDERSTANDING YOUR INCOME TAXES

Ransbottom & Nichol

LuEllen Ransbottom
Former Instructor
Adult and Vocational Education
Ormond Beach, Florida

Fran Moreland Nichol
Freelance Writer
Decatur, Georgia

SOUTH-WESTERN PUBLISHING CO.

Developmental Editor: *Mark Linton*
Senior Production Editor: *Alan Biondi*
Associate Director/Design: *Darren Wright*
Associate Photo Editor/Stylist: *Linda Ellis*
Marketing Manager: *Shelly Battenfield*

Copyright © 1993
by SOUTH-WESTERN PUBLISHING CO.
Cincinnati, Ohio

ISBN: 0-538-70840-9

2 3 4 5 6 7 8 H 99 98 97 96 95 94 93

Printed in the United States of America

 This book is printed on recycled, acid-free paper that meets Environmental Protection Agency standards.

Understanding Your Income Taxes outlines the steps to follow in preparing personal income tax forms. This text-workbook is written specifically for the adult learner and is designed to permit self-paced, individualized instruction and foster student success.

The main focus of *Understanding Your Income Taxes* is on helping students maintain necessary records and understand tax forms. Students learn which forms are best for their individual use, and the steps to follow in preparing these forms.

SPECIAL FEATURES

Understanding Your Income Taxes is designed to help adult learners develop the skills necessary to handle their own personal taxes. Some features of the text-workbook include:

- A larger typeface is used to make the text-workbook easier for the student to read and use. Pages are colorful and uncrowded.

- Competency-based methodology is used. Clear objectives are presented followed by short segments of instruction. These are followed by student activities for immediate reinforcement.

- Content and examples relate to adult-level, real-life issues and skills.

- Pre- and post-tests, with answers and evaluation charts, are included for self-evaluation.

- Study breaks are included to provide refreshing and useful information that contributes to the general literacy of the student.

- Abundant exercises are included, each designed so that the student experiences frequent and meaningful success.

- Goals are listed for each exercise to provide motivation and direction.

- All exercises are supported with Bonus Exercises for the student who needs a second chance to succeed.

- Answers to all exercises are included to facilitate independent, self-paced learning.

- Personal progress is recorded by the student after completing each exercise.

● Individual success is measured by evaluation guides in the student's Personal Progress Record.

INSTRUCTOR'S MANUAL

The Instructor's Manual provides instructional strategies and specific teaching suggestions for *Understanding Your Income Taxes,* along with supplementary bonus exercises and answers, additional testing materials, and a certificate of completion.

Bonus Exercises. A bonus exercise, matching each exercise in the text-workbook, is provided in the manual. These bonus exercises make it possible for students to have a second chance to reach the goals set for each exercise. Answers to the bonus exercises are also provided in the manual. These materials may be reproduced for classroom use.

Testing Materials. Two additional tests, with answers, are provided in the manual to allow for more flexible instruction and evaluation.

Certificate of Completion. Upon completion of *Understanding Your Income Taxes,* a student's success may be recognized through a certificate of completion. This certificate lists the skills and topics covered in this text-workbook. A certificate master is included in the manual.

CONTENTS

Are income taxes a big puzzle to you? Most people have trouble with taxes at one time or another. But you can understand your income tax, and learn to prepare the forms yourself. This book will help you.

You will learn what records to keep and how to keep them. You will learn about the most common tax forms and how to choose the best one for your use. You will have a step-by-step guide to follow in preparing your tax return.

Before you start, meet Rose Anna Valentine. Rose Anna is a single parent raising two children, Buster, six, and Tisha, still in diapers. Rose Anna works hard to make ends meet. She knows it is important to keep records straight. She wants to handle her own income tax returns. Rose Anna will be going through this book with you. When you finish, she will have the skills to manage her record-keeping and her taxes. You will, too!

HOW YOU WILL LEARN

Understanding Your Income Taxes is written with you in mind. You will learn the skills needed to manage your own tax preparation. This book begins with record-keeping information and takes you through steps you can easily follow to handle your own income taxes.

Learn at Your Own Pace

You will progress through the lessons in this book at your own pace. You may move ahead faster, or go slower, than other students. But don't be concerned about this. You are to work at *your* best speed.

Learn Skills Successfully

You are given objectives and goals for each unit. You will know what you are to accomplish. You will study a topic. Then you will complete an exercise. This lets you drill over what you have just learned. When you have shown that you know the topic, you will move on to the next topic. You will always know just how well you are doing as you move through each step in this book.

Complete Bonus Exercises

You may not reach your goal on every practice exercise. When this happens, you should review the lesson and then complete a

Bonus Exercise. These exercises cover the same lessons as the practice exercises in this book. They give you a second chance to reach your goal. When you score higher on a Bonus Exercise than you did on the original activity, you may change your score on your Personal Progress Record. Your instructor has copies of these Bonus Exercises and the answers to them.

Check Your Own Success

You will keep track of your own success. You will check all of your own work. The answers are in the back of this book. The color pages make them easy to find. Always do the exercises *before* you look at the answers. Use the answers as a tool to verify your work —not as a means of filling in the blanks. You will record your scores on your own Personal Progress Record, which is also in the back of this book.

WHAT YOU WILL LEARN ━━━━━━━━━

As you study this book, you will learn how to keep the records you need and how to prepare your income tax returns.

In Unit 1, "Keeping Personal Records," you will learn what income and expense records should be kept. You will learn how to prepare a personal property inventory. You will learn several methods of record-keeping so that you can choose the best one for your use.

In Unit 2, "Understanding Your Taxes," you will learn about tax forms and terms. You will learn how to get ready to file your own taxes and how to choose the right form for you.

In Unit 3, "Preparing Your Tax Return," you will learn, through easy-to-follow steps, how to prepare a Form 1040EZ, a Form 1040A, and a Schedule 2. You will learn how to prepare an Earned Income Tax worksheet.

SPECIAL FEATURES ━━━━━━━━━━━

Understanding Your Income Taxes has a number of special features. These features will help you learn and apply the material successfully.

Checking What You Know

You can check what you already know about budgeting time and money before you start studying this book. Checking What You Know lets you know what skills you need to improve upon. Then, when you complete this book, you will do an exercise called *Checking What You Have Learned.* By comparing these two scores you will see how much you have gained through your study.

Making Your Money Work for You

This book has special features designed to give you a break from the regular study. These breaks have interesting stories about your money and helpful hints for making your money work for you.

Putting It Together

Each unit has a number of short exercises called *Checkpoints.* These exercises will help you check your understanding of a specific topic before continuing. At the end of each unit you will find a section titled *Putting It Together.* This section contains several exercises that are similar to the Checkpoints. They will help you to reinforce the skills you learned in each unit.

Personal Progress Record

You will keep track of your own progress. Once you check your answers, you will record your score on your Personal Progress Record at the end of this book. After you finish a unit, you will be able to see your level of success.

Completion Certificate

When you finish your study in this book you may be eligible for a certificate of completion. Your instructor will explain to you the skill level required for this award.

READY TO START

You are now ready to start learning to understand your income tax. You will find the skills you learn through this book can help you in many ways.

Preparing a personal property inventory can help you when you move or if you should have an insurance claim. Keeping good records can help you with your job or when you need government assistance. And preparing your own tax return is a skill you can learn.

Turn to page xiii and complete Checking What You Know. Check your answers with the answers on page 53. Then begin Unit 1, "Keeping Personal Records."

LuEllen Ransbottom
Fran Moreland Nichol

CHECKING WHAT YOU KNOW

Take this pre-test before starting *Understanding Your Income Taxes*. The 20 questions will tell you how much you already know about income taxes. They will also tell you what you need to learn.

There is no time limit, so take your time. When you finish, check your answers. Give yourself 1 point for each correct answer. Record you score on your Personal Progress Record. After finishing the book, you will be able to see how much you learned.

DIRECTIONS: Each statement is either true or false. Write *T* (true) or *F* (false) in the space provided.

_____ 1. A Form W-4 is given to a wage earner to show the amount of money earned and taxes withheld during the year.

_____ 2. Careful record keeping of income and expenses will save time when preparing your income tax return.

_____ 3. A bank will furnish a Form 1099-INT if it has paid you any interest during the year.

_____ 4. A receipt is written proof of purchase.

_____ 5. A seller's guarantee of the quality of an item is a warranty.

_____ 6. A list of the items you own is called a property profile.

_____ 7. Keeping a record of the model number on an appliance is not helpful when it needs repair.

_____ 8. Taxes are monies collected to help pay for services the government provides.

_____ 9. The Pentagon is the agency responsible for collecting federal income taxes.

_____ 10. The amount of income tax you must pay depends on your gross income.

_____ 11. Social security taxes are called FICA on tax forms.

_____ 12. You may claim an exemption for yourself, your spouse, and each person who qualifies as your dependent.

_____ 13. Income tax forms and payments must be mailed before May 15 of the year after you earned income.

_____ 14. If you provide more than 50% of the expense of someone else, that person is your spouse.

_____ 15. The simplest tax form is the 1040 EZ.

_____ 16. You must add a Schedule 1 to your 1040A tax form if you have earned $400 or more in taxable interest.

_____ 17. "Head of household" is a filing status.

_____ 18. A credit for child care cannot be taken on a Schedule 2.

_____ 19. When you have paid in more taxes than are due, you are entitled to file your tax return late.

_____ 20. Earned income credit is a refund given to certain workers with low income.

☞ *Check Your work on page 53. Record your score on page 59.*

UNIT 1

Keeping Personal Records

WHAT YOU WILL LEARN

When you finish this unit, you will be able to:

- Identify three types of income records that must be kept.
- Identify three types of expense records that must be kept.
- Prepare a personal property inventory.
- Identify two methods of keeping records.

Rose Anna Valentine knows that keeping track of personal records is important. Like most of us, she has never taken the time to get organized. Pulling together important personal records takes time.

One day, Rose Anna said, "I am going to get my personal records organized! I'm tired of not knowing where these important papers are when I need them." Buster Valentine was helping his mom, Rose Anna, with her papers. "I have my bank statements and daily logs of our expenses for the past two months," she said to Buster. "The daily log has helped me watch our expenses. But now we need to put all these forms, bills, and receipts in one place."

INCOME AND EXPENSE RECORDS

Records need to be kept for several reasons. One very important reason is for tax purposes. Careful record keeping of income and expenses will save you time when preparing your income tax returns.

The expense receipts or income documents are proof of what you have earned and spent. You will need them if you have insurance claims, if you are involved in a dispute, or for tax purposes. A **dispute** is a disagreement between you and someone else. If someone wrongly says you have not paid a bill, your receipt will settle that dispute.

Many documents you keep will never be needed. But for your own protection, you should learn to keep them. That way, when there *is* a need, you won't have to worry.

Income Records

Income records that you need to keep are (1) Form W-2, Wage and Tax Statement, and (2) Form 1099-INT, a statement of interest earned. The first form will come to you from your employer. The second form will come to you from your bank. A copy of your Form W-2 must be attached to your income tax return. The amount of interest recorded on your Form 1099-INT must be recorded on your income tax return.

Form W-2, Wage and Tax Statement.

Form W-2 is a form prepared by your employer and given to you by January 31 of the year following the year in which you worked. For example, you will receive your 1993 Form W-2 by January 31, 1994. Form W-2 shows money earned and deductions made for the past year. **Deductions** are amounts subtracted from your gross pay. One of these deductions is for social security taxes. City, state, and federal tax deductions are shown on Form W-2, also.

Keep your paycheck stubs all year until you receive your Form W-2. Add your paycheck stubs and compare with your Form W-2. If you find an error, report it to your employer immediately.

Form 1099-INT.

Your bank will furnish a Form 1099-INT statement of interest earned on your savings account. You may also receive interest on your checking account. If you earned over $100 dollars of interest in one year, you must record that amount on your income tax return. The bank sends a copy of your Form 1099-INT to the Internal Revenue Service (IRS), too. The IRS will match your return with the Form 1099s received with your name and social security number to be sure you properly recorded your interest earnings.

Illustration 1-1

Careful record keeping of income and expenses will save you time when preparing your income tax returns.

Expense Records

Expense records need to be kept for insurance and tax purposes. Important expense records are (1) medical bills, (2) charity contributions, (3) work-related expenses, (4) living expenses, and (5) major purchases.

Medical Bills

All medical bills, receipts, prescription sales tickets, or related documents, should be kept together. A **receipt** is documentation of payment made. Bills or receipts from your pharmacy are as important as those from your doctor.

Charity Contributions

A **charity** is an organization or fund to help those in need. When you give money to your church or charity, you should ask for a receipt. If you give cash and do not get a receipt, keep a note listing the charity and the amount given.

Work-Related Expenses

You should keep records on anything you spend to help with your work. Tools, supplies, equipment, uniforms, or training classes would be some examples.

Living Expenses

Keep receipts for rent, housing expenses (such as repairs and maintenance), payments on loans, charge accounts, and utility bills.

Major Purchases

Keep receipts for major purchases such as furniture and appliances. You need to know the value of your household items to be sure you have enough property insurance.

CHECKPOINT 1-1

YOUR GOAL:
Get 4 or more points.

Read carefully the statements below. Fill in the correct word or words to complete each sentence in the space provided. Use the words listed below. An example is done for you.

- A ___Form W-2___ shows money earned and deductions made through the year.

1. All medical _____ should be kept together.

2. A refrigerator is a _____.

3. A _____ is an organization or fund to help those in need.

4. Records of tools, supplies, and other _____ should be kept.

5. A receipt is documentation of _____.

6. Banks will furnish _____ for interest earned.

work-related expenses
bills and receipts
major purchase
Form W-2
charity
payment made
Form 1099-INT

☞ *Check your work on page 53. Record your score on page 60.*

PREPARING A PERSONAL PROPERTY INVENTORY

An **inventory** is a list of items in your possession. It can be useful if you have a loss through fire, theft, or property damage. Your inventory can also help when you need proof of ownership for any other reason. Keep your inventory to document value if something is lost or if you want to sell something you own. Include photographs of all major items with your inventory.

When you prepare your personal property inventory, make an extra copy that can be kept at work or in a safe place. Review it at least once a year. You may want to set aside a day, such as your birthday, to update your inventory every year.

What to Include in Your Inventory

Not everything needs to be included in your inventory. Inexpensive jewelry or personal items can be left out, or can be recorded as a group. You can also list clothing in groups, such as "6 sweaters, $60." Some of the things to include in a personal property inventory are:

1. *Furniture and Appliances*. A list of major purchases will be all you need. If you buy something like a new washing machine, add it to the list. Keep the model number, serial number, and any other information that will help if you need a repair later. Record the date of purchase and full amount paid for each item.
2. *Radios, TVs, Cameras, Etc*. These are the things most often stolen. You need good records to prove that you owned the stolen items.
3. *Special Possessions*. Keep descriptions and registration numbers of bicycles; keep information that could help you identify any other items of value you have.

Showing Proof of Ownership

Proof of ownership is written verification that an item belongs to you. Keeping correct records will allow you to prove ownership whenever you need to do so. Some of the information to include in your personal property inventory in order to show proof of ownership includes the following:

1. *Item*. Record the item such as chair or watch.
2. *Identification*. Record the manufacturer, or where you purchased the item. Record the serial number or model number, and any special markings or details.
3. *Year Purchased*. Record the date you purchased the item. If you do not know, write down when you think it was purchased.
4. *Purchase Price*. Record the price you paid. If the item was a gift, write down what you think it cost when purchased.

5. *Approximate Current Value.* Record what you think the item is worth now. Has it been damaged or badly used? If so, its approximate current value will be less.

6. *Warranties.* A **warranty** is a guarantee of quality given by the seller or manufacturer. When you buy a product, such as a stereo or a toaster oven, it will come with a written warranty. The warranty says the product will do what it is supposed to do or the seller or manufacturer will replace or repair the product. It does not protect against normal wear and tear; but it protects against defects. A **defect** is something wrong with a product. Warranties should be noted on your personal property inventory. That way, if something breaks, you will know whether you are protected.

7. *Photographs.* Take pictures of items on your inventory and keep them together. Photos are good proof of ownership.

CHECKPOINT 1-2

YOUR GOAL:
Get 4 or more points.

Read carefully the following statements. Each statement is either true or false. Write T (true) or F (false) in the space provided. An example is done for you.

___T___ ● An inventory can help provide proof of ownership.

_____ 1. Radios, TVs, and cameras are among personal items most often stolen.

_____ 2. It is not important to keep model numbers.

_____ 3. A warranty protects against normal wear and tear.

_____ 4. Proof of ownership may be useful if property is lost through fire or theft.

_____ 5. Approximate current value is the amount originally paid for an item.

☞ *Check your work on page 53. Record your score on page 60.*

Rose Anna took a piece of paper out of Buster's notebook to make her personal property inventory. The inventory she wrote out is shown in Illustration 1-2.

A	B	C	D	E	F
Item	Identification	Year Purchased	Purchase Price	Approximate Current Value	Warranty
A-1 Portable TV	Serial # 000111222	1990	$595.00	$400.00	24 mos.
Wedding ring	gold band	1984	---	$150.00	
3-piece maple bedroom suite		1988	$400.00	$200.00	
boy's Tuff-made bike	10# xxyyzz	1989	$80.00	$50.00	
Toastee Toaster Oven	#445566	1987	$29.00	$15.00	

Illustration 1-2

Rose Anna's Personal Property Inventory

MAKING YOUR MONEY WORK FOR YOU

One way to make your money work for you is to keep your possessions from getting stolen. Often, thieves will pass up an item that could be easily identified. Most police departments have an engraving tool citizens can borrow. You can use this tool to mark items like TV sets and stereos with your social security number. If your police department does not have an engraving tool, scratch your social security number on the bottom with a pin or sharp knife. If something you own is lost or stolen, you can help find it.

RECORD-KEEPING METHODS

It is important to keep records in one place. You do not need an expensive cabinet. Choose a storage container that can be kept in a dry place and is easy to reach.

File Boxes

One way to set up a record system is with a file box. You can purchase an inexpensive file box at a discount store. You will only need a few files to keep your records properly. Rose Anna decided to keep her personal records in a file box. Rose Anna's file box is shown in Illustration 1-3.

Illustration 1-3

Rose Anna's
File Box

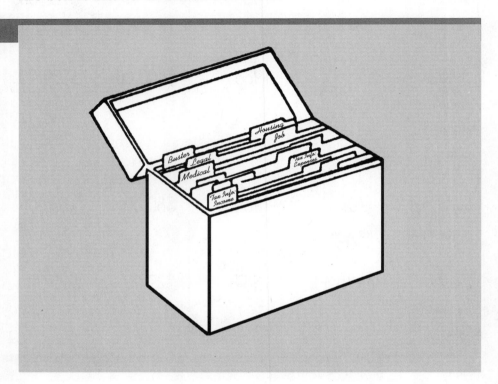

Once you have a box and set of file folders, choose the main topics you will need. Make a file for each one. Put these in alphabetic order. Your personal files might include the following:

1. *Bank Statements and Personal Checks*. Keep all statements and checks together in order of date.

2. *Car*. Keep records of repairs and expenses. Keep receipts for gas used for your work.

3. *Children*. Set up a file for each child. It is useful to keep medical records such as dates of illnesses and vaccinations. You may also want to keep school records.

4. *Furniture and Equipment*. Keep receipts of any major purchases. Keep information concerning repair or maintenance that comes with purchases.

5. *Housing*. Rent receipts or records of other payments for household expenses go in this folder. Also keep copies of your lease agreement.

6. *Insurance Policies and Premium Receipts*. Keep copies of any insurance policies you own and receipts of payments made.

7. *Job*. Information about your work should be kept in this folder. Also keep receipts of expenses you have that are a part of your work. Keep names of employers, supervisors, or others you may later want to contact. Keep information that may be needed when applying for another job.

8. *Legal Papers*. Immigration papers, divorce papers, or records of any court procedures that have concerned you.

9. *Medical*. Keep receipts for visits to the doctor, dentist, or clinic. Keep receipts for all medicines or medical supplies.

10. *Tax Information: Income*. In this folder, keep Form W-2s and other income records.

11. *Tax Information: Expenses*. In this folder, keep receipts of contributions to charity or other documents showing tax-related expenses.

12. *Utilities*. Records of utility deposits, agreements, and payments of monthly bills go in this folder.

13. *Warranties and Instructions*. Keep warranties that come with appliances and equipment. Keep instructions concerning installation, maintenance, and replacement.

If you have a checking account, your canceled checks will serve as proof of payment for such things as rent and utilities. If you do not have a checking account, be sure to keep receipts for these and other payments for which you need proof.

✔ CHECKPOINT 1-3

YOUR GOAL:
Get 4 or more points.

Yu-lan is setting up his personal files. He has labeled six files. Put each of the following items into the correct file for Yu-lan. Choose from the files listed below. Write your answer in the space provided. An example is done for you.

Item   File

● Instructions for toaster/oven   *Furniture and Equipment*

1. Bills for job tools   _____

2. Receipt for headache prescription   _____

3. Electric bills   _____

4. Copy of apartment lease   _____

5. Form W-2s   _____

Furniture and Equipment
Housing
Medical bills
Tax Information: Income
Tax Information: Expense
Utilities

👉 *Check your work on page 53. Record your score on page 60.*

Expanding File ━━━━━━━━━━

Most general stores and discount stores have an expanding file made of heavy paper. This is a simple and inexpensive way to keep personal records. Rose Anna's friend Angela kept her records in an expanding file. Angela's file is shown in Illustration 1-4.

If you choose this method of record keeping, follow these three steps to set up your file:

1. Make a list of the topics you will need.
2. Put them in alphabetic order.
3. Label sections of your expanding file to match. Leave a section or two in between each label so you will have room to add other sections later.

Illustration 1-4

Expanding
File

Other Filing Methods

You can keep personal records together in other inexpensive ways, using a shoe box, plastic box, or large manila envelope. Set up your records using the categories listed under File Boxes.

WHAT YOU HAVE LEARNED

After studying this unit you have learned to:

- Identify income records to be kept.
- Identify expense records to be kept.
- Prepare a personal property inventory.
- Set up a personal records file.

ACTIVITY 1-1   YOUR GOAL: Get 5 or more points.

Set up your own personal records system. From the files listed on pages 8-9, choose the ones that apply to you. Add any other subjects your family may need. List the files that you will need in the space provided. An example is done for you.

● _Housing_ _____

1. _____

2. _____

3. _____

4. _____

5. _____

6. _____

7. _____

☞ *Check your work on page 53. Record your score on page 60.*

ACTIVITY 1-2   YOUR GOAL: Get 10 or more points.

Use the form on the next page to prepare your own personal property inventory. Write the information about items you own in the space provided.

A	B	C	D	E	F
		Year	Purchase	Approximate	
Item	Identification	Purchased	Price	Current Value	Warranty

☞ *Check your work on page 53. Record your score on page 60.*

ACTIVITY 1-3   YOUR GOAL: Get 9 or more points.

Read the following story carefully. At the end of the story is a list of files. Put each item in the story in its correct file. Write the number assigned to the item in the space provided. More than one item may go into a file. An example is done for you.

Mario and Imelda are doing their filing for January. They just received Mario's Form W-2 (1) and another Form W-2 (2) showing money Imelda received for some part-time work. They also received a Form 1099-INT (3) from their bank showing a small amount of interest earned on their special checking account. Mario gave $5.00 in January to a church collection (4). Imelda also gave some money to a charity fund drive (5). Imelda spent money on flu shots (6) and on some medicine (7). Mario had receipts for some tools he bought for his job (8) and for an instructional manual (9) he needed. They paid for a tune-up on the family car (10) and made a payment on the refrigerator (11).

● _____11_____   **Furniture and Equipment**

1. _____   **Car Expenses**

2. _____   **Tax Information: Income**

3. _____   **Job-Related Expenses**

4. _____   **Medical and Pharmacy Bills**

5. _____   **Tax Information Expenses**

☞ *Check your work on page 53. Record your score on page 60.*

UNIT 2

Understanding Your Taxes

WHAT YOU WILL LEARN:

When you finish this unit, you will be able to:

- Define terms used on income tax forms.
- Identify five parts of a Form W-2.
- Know when to file and who must file income tax returns.
- Choose the proper tax form for your use.

Rose Anna opened her mailbox one day in late January. She found an envelope from Discount Mart. The small piece of paper inside had W-2 printed at the top. "Tax time must be getting close," Rose Anna thought.

Rose Anna had always gotten someone to help her with taxes. But this year, she thought, it would be different. This year she would do it herself. In this unit, you and Rose Anna will learn to prepare income tax forms.

UNDERSTANDING TAXES AND TERMS

Like Rose Anna, you may wonder why we pay taxes on money we earn. Income taxes have been paid in the U.S. since 1913. During the Great Depression of the 1930s many people lost their jobs or their savings. There were no welfare or unemployment programs. In 1935, the Social Security Act was passed, creating the Internal Revenue Service (IRS). The IRS collects taxes and passes this money on to the government. Your taxes then help pay for programs that help all U.S. citizens.

The government does not send you an income tax bill. It is your responsibility to prepare your tax return and pay your taxes.

Taxes are monies collected to help pay for services the government provides. One major source of taxes is the income tax. The **income tax** is a certain amount of money paid to the government based on the amount of income for that year. Almost all workers in this country pay income taxes. The **Internal Revenue Service** (IRS) is the agency responsible for collecting income taxes.

To understand IRS forms, you need to know some of the most commonly used terms. Some of these terms are:

Wages. Monies paid for work done.

Dependent. Someone who relies on you for support. Your child is your *dependent*. If you provide more than 50 percent of the expense of someone else, such as an elderly parent or another family member, that person is also a dependent.

Exemption. An allowance a taxpayer claims for each dependent. Exemptions reduce your taxable income. You may claim an exemption for yourself, your spouse, and each person who qualifies as your dependent.

Non-employee compensation. Money paid to a worker who is not a regular employee. Payment for contract work (such as painting a house) or for other work when you are not on a payroll would be non-employee compensation. Taxes are not withheld on this kind of wages, but you are still responsible for paying those taxes.

Withhold. To take out, or hold out money. When your employer pays your wages, he or she *withholds* a certain amount for taxes.

Income. The amount of money paid to you during a period of time. Your *total income* is the money you receive from all sources, including wages, salaries, tips, interest, unemployment compensation, and other benefits.

Social Security Administration. A federal agency set up to provide for wage earners when they reach the age

Illustration 2-1

The Internal
Revenue
Service is the
agency
responsible for
collecting
income taxes.

of 65 or become unable to work. When you pay social
security taxes, that money is set aside in a special
account. Social security taxes are called FICA on tax
forms. FICA stands for Federal Insurance Contributions
Act of 1935. All you need to remember is that social
security and FICA are the same.

Taxable Income. Your income less exemption allowances, deductions, and tax credits. Your taxable income
is the amount you use to figure your taxes.

CHECKPOINT 2-1

Read the definitions below carefully and fill in the blank with the correct word to match the definition. Use the words given below. An example is done for you.

● _Withhold_   To take out, or hold out money.

1. _____   Someone who relies on you for support.

2. _____   A federal agency set up to provide for wage earners when they reach the age of 65 or become unable to work.

3. _____   Monies paid for work done.

4. _____   Monies collected to pay for services the government provides.

5. _____   An allowance a taxpayer claims for each dependent.

6. _____   The agency responsible for collecting income taxes.

withhold
wages
Social Security Administration
taxes
Internal Revenue Service
exemption
dependent

☞ *Check your work on page 53. Record your score on page 60.*

FORM W-2

The Form W-2 you receive from your employer after the first of the year includes most of the tax information you need. A sample Form W-2 is shown in Illustration 2-2

To help you identify some of the boxes most commonly used for federal income tax purposes, they are explained below and numbered the same as in Illustration 2-2.

Illustration 2-2

Rose Anna's
Form W-2.

1 Control number											
		OMB No. 1545–0008									
2 Employer's name, address, and ZIP code			6 Statutory employee	Deceased	Pension plan	Legal rep.	942 emp.	Subtotal	Deferred compensation		Void
DISCOUNT MART, INC. 2602 E. Tenth St. Ormond Beach, FL 32174-2612			☐	☐	☐	☐	☐	☐	☐		☐
			7 Allocated tips				8 Advanced EIC payment				
			9 Federal income tax withheld $144				10 Wages, tips, other compensation $14,440				
3 Employer's identification number 67-8004646	4 Employer's state I.D. number		11 Social security tax withheld $1,044				12 Social security wages $14,440				
5 Employer's social security number 437-00-2111			13 Social security tips				14 Nonqualified plans				
19 Employee's name, address and ZIP code			15 Dependent care benefits				16 Fringe benefits incl. in Box 10				
ROSE ANNA VALENTINE 1765 Sheridan Drive Apartment 3 Ormond Beach, FL 32174-1234			17				18 Other				

Box 2. Your employer's name and address are in the upper left portion of your Form W-2.

Box 3. Your employer's identification number (EIN), is in the upper right portion. This is the number your employer uses for all tax reporting.

Box 5. Your social security number. Always verify that it is correct.

Box 7. If your income is all, or primarily, from tips, your employer may furnish you with a Form W-2 showing _Allocated Tips_. Major food and beverage firms are required to do this. Your employer will fill in an amount that is based on 8 percent of the business' gross receipts. For example, if you are the only waiter in a restaurant that has $1,000 in gross receipts, your employer may furnish you with a Form W-2 listing $80 in tips.

You have the right to dispute the figure in Box 7. If you think you did not earn that much money in tips, you can say so.

You will need proof, though. The best way to do this is with a daily log. Every working day, write down the amount of tips you actually receive. The IRS will usually accept your daily log, if it is clearly written and well kept.

Box 9. The total amount of federal income tax withheld.

Box 10. Wages, tips, and other compensation paid to you by this employer. Keep your own records of wages, tips, and other compensation paid to you. Check your records against the figure in Box 10 to make sure it is correct.

Box 11. The total amount of social security taxes withheld. Forms W-2 are also used for state and local income tax purposes, and boxes are provided for that information. You will only be working with information provided for federal taxes in this Unit.

Box 12. Social security wages are in a separate box. These are the wages from which social security taxes have been withheld. Usually, the social security wages will be the same amount as the total wages paid.

Box 19. Your name, address, and ZIP Code. Always verify that these are correct.

CHECKPOINT 2-2

YOUR GOAL:
Get 4 or more points.

Read carefully the information below. Using the information given, fill in the correct spaces in the Form W-2. An example is done for you.

1 Control number		
	OMB No. 1545–0008	
2 Employer's name, address, and ZIP code		**6** Statutory employee ☐ Deceased ☐ Pension plan ☐ Legal rep. ☐ 942 emp. ☐ Subtotal ☐ Deferred compensation ☐ Void ☐
		7 Allocated tips	**8** Advanced EIC payment
		9 Federal income tax withheld	**10** Wages, tips, other compensation
3 Employer's identification number	**4** Employer's state I.D. number	**11** Social security tax withheld	**12** Social security wages
5 Employer's social security number		**13** Social security tips	**14** Nonqualified plans
19 Employee's name, address and ZIP code Felix Herrera		**15** Dependent care benefits	**16** Fringe benefits incl. in Box 10
		17	**18** Other

- Felix Herrera is the employee.
1. Felix's social security number is 111-22-3333.
2. Felix lives at 499 Hawthorn St., San Diego, CA 92101-6784.
3. Felix works for All-Rite Tool Shop, 4764 Industrial Road, San Diego, CA 92121-2405.
4. Felix's total wages were $14,560.
5. Social security tax withheld was $1,113.84.
6. Federal tax withheld was $840.

☞ **Check your work on page 53. Record your score on page 60.**

MAKING YOUR MONEY WORK FOR YOU

You can get free help with your taxes. You can call IRS toll-free from any of the fifty states. Look in the U.S. Government section of your telephone book, under Internal Revenue Service — IRS. IRS will not prepare your return for you. But there is a volunteer program that will help you. Volunteer Income Tax Assistance (VITA) helps prepare simple tax forms or answers questions. VITA programs are located in malls, libraries, and other convenient places. Call the IRS toll-free number for the program nearest you!

GETTING READY TO FILE YOUR TAXES

If you keep good records all year, filing your income tax will be easier. Make sure all of your income and expense information is in one place. Then you have three questions to consider: (1) when to file, (2) who must file, and (3) which form to use.

When to File

It is your responsibility to file your tax return each year. You do not receive a bill or reminder from the government.

Income tax forms must be mailed before April 15 of the year after you earned income. If April 15 is on a weekend or on a holiday, your tax return is due the following workday. You can be charged penalties for late filing.

Who Must File

The amount of income determines who must file an income tax return. Which persons and income levels are listed below.

Single or widowed persons	with gross income of
under 65	$ 5,100
65 or over	$ 5,850

Married persons filing joint return	with gross income of
both spouses under 65	$ 9, 200
both spouses 65 or older	$10,400

There are other conditions that could affect whether or not you must file a tax return. These conditions have to do with your age and family. It is always best to file a return, even if you think you may not have made enough money.

CHOOSING YOUR TAX FORM

There are three tax forms from which to choose: (1) Form 1040EZ, (2) Form 1040A, and (3) Form 1040. Read the list under each form to determine which form you should use.

Form 1040EZ

Form 1040EZ is the form to use if you meet all of the following conditions:

1. You are single and not over 65 or blind.
2. You will claim no more than one personal exemption.
3. You have taxable income of less than $50,000.
4. You have no more than $400 income from interest; all other income is from wages, salaries, tips, and taxable scholarships or fellowships.
5. You have no adjustments to income, no itemized deductions, no other taxes, and no tax credits.

Form 1040A

Form 1040A is the form to use if you meet the following conditions:

1. You are single, married (filing jointly or separately), or head of household.
2. You have taxable income of less than $50,000.
3. You have income from wages, salaries, tips, interest, dividends, or unemployment compensation.
4. You have no itemized deductions.
5. You may have a deductible IRA contribution.
6. You have no tax credits except child and dependent care and/or earned income credit.

Form 1040

Form 1040 is the form to use if you meet any of the following conditions:

1. You are a qualifying widow(er) with dependent child.
2. Your income exceeds $50,000.
3. You received taxable social security or railroad retirement benefits, self-employment earnings, rents and royalties, or income from pensions and annuities.
4. You had taxable state and local tax refunds, capital gains, gain from sale of your house, alimony income, or income from other sources.

5. Your adjustments to income include alimony paid, penalty for early withdrawal of savings, reimbursed employee business expenses, or other adjustments.

6. You want to itemize deductions such as state and local income taxes, contributions to charity, medical and dental expenses, losses from casualty or theft, moving expenses, and miscellaneous deductions.

7. You have other taxes due, such as self-employment or social security tax on tips.

8. Your tax credits include foreign tax credit, credit for elderly, or other credits of this sort.

CHECKPOINT 2-3

YOUR GOAL: Get 5 or more points.

Read carefully the statements below. Write the correct word or words in the space provided. Use the words in the list below. An example is done for you.

workday	**$10,400**
itemized deductions	**April 15**
income and expense	**$5,100**
Form 1040	**penalties**

● Income tax forms must be mailed before _April 15_____.

1. If you are single, under 65, and have a gross income of

   _____ or more, you must file a tax return.

2. If April 15 is on a weekend or holiday, your tax return is due

   the following _____.

3. Before starting to prepare your taxes, you should have all

   _____ records ready.

4. Married persons filing jointly must file a tax return if both

   spouses are over 65 and have a gross income of

   _____ or more.

5. If you have taxable income of less than $50,000, no

   _____, and tax credits only for child and

   dependent care, you should use Form 1040A.

workday	**$10,400**
itemized deductions	**April 15**
income and expense	**$5,100**
Form 1040	**penalties**

6. You can be charged _____ for late filing of

   your tax return.

7. If you have tax credits including foreign tax credit or credit

   for elderly, you should use _____.

☞ *Check your work on page 54. Record your score on page 60.*

WHAT YOU HAVE LEARNED

After studying this unit, you have learned to:

● Define five terms used on income tax forms.
● Identify five parts of a Form W-2.
● Know when to file and who must file income tax returns.
● Choose the proper tax form for your use.

ACTIVITY 2-1   YOUR GOAL: Get 5 or more points.

Use the Form W-2 below to find the information requested. Write your answers
in the spaces provided. An example is done for you.

1 Control number									
		OMB No. 1545–0008							

2 Employer's name, address, and ZIP code	6 Statutory employee	Deceased	Pension plan	Legal rep.	942 emp.	Subtotal	Deferred compensation	Void
S & S FOUNDRY 578 Peachtree Drive Atlanta, GA 30305-6432	☐	☐	☐	☐	☐	☐	☐	☐

	7 Allocated tips	8 Advanced EIC payment

	9 Federal income tax withheld $2,174.32	10 Wages, tips, other compensation $16,275.88

3 Employer's identification number 22-4466990	4 Employer's state I.D. number	11 Social security tax withheld $1,245.10	12 Social security wages $16,275.88
5 Employer's social security number 407-66-8389		13 Social security tips	14 Nonqualified plans
19 Employee's name, address and ZIP code Jason Greenfield 71 Sutton St. Atlanta, GA 30317-4526		15 Dependent care benefits	16 Fringe benefits incl. in Box 10
		17	18 Other

● What is the employer's identification number? _22-4466990_____

1. What is the employee's name? _____

2. What is the employee's social security number? _____

3. What is the total amount paid to this employee? _____

4. How much federal income tax was withheld? _____

5. How much social security tax was withheld? _____

6. What is the name of the hiring company? _____

☞ *Check your work on page 54. Record your score on page 60.*

25

ACTIVITY 2-2   YOUR GOAL: Get 5 or more points.

Read the conditions regarding each taxpayer listed below. Decide if the taxpayer should file a Form 1040EZ, Form 1040A, Form 1040, or none. Write your answer in the space provided. An example is done for you.

1040EZ
1040A
1040
None

●   _1040A_____   Taxpayer is head of household with income of $16,000 and has a tax credit for child care.

1. _____   Taxpayer is a 35-year-old single person with no dependents, no itemized deductions, and income from wages in the amount of $24,000.

2. _____   Taxpayer wants to itemize deductions for charity contributions.

3. _____   Taxpayer is a 60-year-old widow with a taxable gross income of under $50,000.

4. _____   Taxpayer is single with two dependents and has a taxable income of under $50,000.

5. _____   Taxpayer receives income from pensions and annuities.

6. _____   Taxpayer is married filing a joint return with an income of $10,000. Both spouses are 67 years of age.

7. _____   Taxpayer is married with a taxable income from wages of $22,000 and interest income of $200. Taxpayer has no itemized deductions or tax credits.

☞   *Check your work on page 54. Record your score on page 60.*

UNIT 3

Preparing Your Tax Return

WHAT YOU WILL LEARN

When you finish this unit, you will be able to:

- Prepare Form 1040EZ.
- Prepare Form 1040A.
- Prepare Schedule 2: Credit for Child and Dependent Care Expenses for Form 1040A Filers.
- Prepare an Earned Income Credit Worksheet.

Rose Anna was ready to prepare her tax return. She and her friend Georgina set aside a Saturday to work together. They could help each other. So Georgina brought her files over and they sat down at the kitchen table.

Rose Anna used Form 1040A. She needed Form 1040A because of her dependents, Tisha and Buster. Georgina used Form 1040EZ. She could use Form 1040EZ because she does not have any dependents.

Rose Anna and Georgina went through their forms step by step. In just a short time they had completed their forms. You can too!

PREPARING FORM 1040EZ

As it sounds, Form 1040EZ is the easy form to use. If you meet the conditions to use Form 1040EZ, you will need less time and effort to prepare your tax return.

Rose Anna and Georgina decided to prepare Georgina's return first. They followed the steps outlined below. Refer to Georgina's return in Illustration 3-1 as you read the steps.

Illustration 3-1

Georgina's Form 1040EZ

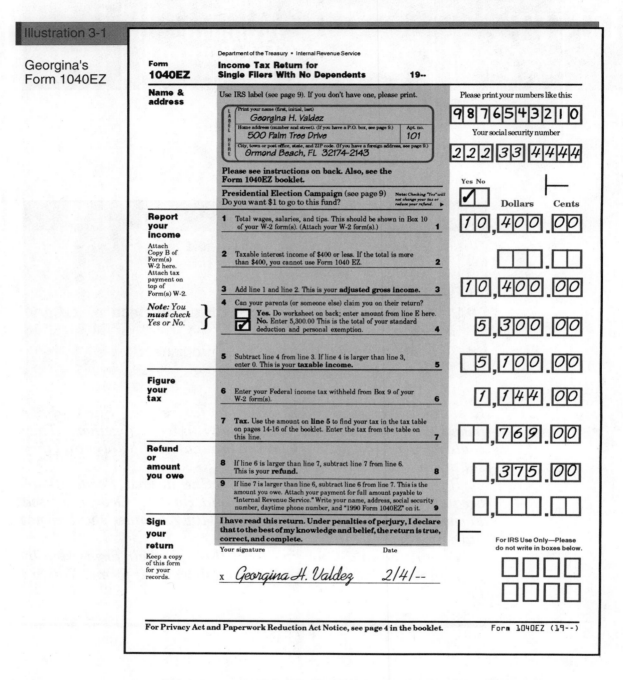

Get what you will need ready ahead of time, like the person pictured in Illustration 3-2. Instructions for preparing Form 1040EZ are on the back of the form. The steps to follow are listed on the next two pages.

Illustration 3-2

If you meet the conditions to use Form 1040EZ, you will need less time and effort to prepare your tax return.

1. *Name and Address.* Print your name, address, and social security number clearly in the spaces provided. Check the Yes box if you want $1 to go to the Presidential Election Campaign Fund. The dollar will come out of taxes already withheld. It is not an additional tax.

2. *Report Your Income.* On line 1 enter your total wages, salaries, and tips. Enter the figure that is shown on your Form W-2. Copies of your Form W-2 must be attached to your return. On line 2 enter taxable interest income of $400 or less. If your total taxable interest income was more than $400 you cannot use Form 1040EZ.

   Add lines 1 and 2 to get your *adjusted gross income.* Enter this figure on line 3. Your total income minus any allowable adjustments is your **adjusted gross income.**

   For line 4, ask yourself if you are a dependent on someone else's tax return (such as your parent's). If so, check Yes. Then complete the worksheet on the back of the form to determine the amount of standard deduction allowed. If you check No, enter the amount of your standard deduction ($5,300). For line 5, subtract line 4 from line 3.

3. *Figure Your Tax.* Enter your Federal income tax withheld on line 6. Enter the amount shown in Box 9 of your Form W-2.

   Use the amount on line 5 to find your tax in the tax table. Look up your tax in the tax table in the instruction book. Enter the tax amount on line 7.

4. *Refund or Amount You Owe.* If line 6 is larger than line 7, subtract line 7 from line 6. The is your *refund*. Enter this amount on line 8. Your **refund** is a payment given back to you.

  If line 7 is larger that line 6, subtract line 6 from line 7. This is the amount you owe. Enter this amount on line 9. Be sure to attach your *check or money order* for the full amount shown on line 9. Make it payable to *Internal Revenue Service*. Write your name, address, social security number, daytime phone number, and Form 1040EZ on your payment. Also write the year for which these taxes are being paid.

5. *Sign Your Return.* Make sure all the Forms W-2 you received are attached.

MAKING YOUR MONEY WORK FOR YOU

Do you have a question for IRS? IRS wants to give you an answer. The agency has set up a toll-free number you can call with questions on more than 140 subjects. Tele-Tax numbers have information on everything from child care credit to tips. Look in your tax instruction booklet (or pick up an instruction book at the Post Office) to find out how to call Tele-Tax.

CHECKPOINT 3-1

YOUR GOAL:
Get 4 or more points.

Read carefully the Form 1040EZ prepared by Georgina Valdez shown in Illustration 3-1 on page 28. Read carefully the sentences below. Fill in the blanks with the correct answer from Georgina's Form 1040EZ. Use the words listed below. An example is done for you.

$1,144.00	No
Line 8	Yes
$10,400.00	$769.00
top right corner	

- Georgina's social security number is entered in the blocks in the _top right corner_ of Form 1040EZ.

1. Georgina will be getting a tax refund. Her refund is listed on _____.

2. Georgina's total wages for the year were

_____.

3. Georgina wanted $1 to go to the Presidential Election Campaign fund. She indicated that by placing a check mark in the _____ box at the top of the page.

4. The total Federal income tax withheld by Georgina's employer, and shown on her Form W-2 was

_____.

5. Her parents could not claim Georgina on their return. She checked the _____ box on line 4.

6. Georgina's total tax for the year was _____.

☞ **Check your work on page 54. Record your score on page 60.**

PREPARING FORM 1040A AND SCHEDULE 2

Form 1040A is printed on the front and back sides of one sheet of paper. There are separate sheets to fill out and attach to Form 1040A for three different circumstances:

Schedule 1   Interest and Dividend Income. Complete this form if you have over $400 in taxable interest.

Schedule 2   Child and Dependent Care. Complete this form if you are claiming child and dependent credit.

Schedule 3   Credit for the Elderly or the Disabled. Complete this form if you were 65 or older at the end of the tax year, or if you are disabled.

Schedule 2 is explained in more detail beginning on page 35. More information on all three schedules is included in the Form 1040A instruction booklet.

Before starting to prepare your Form 1040A, have all of your information ready. You will need your Forms W-2. You will also need all of your income and expense records.

When you have all of your information, follow the step-by-step instructions on the Form 1040A. Refer to Form 1040A in Illustration 3-3 as you follow the steps on pages 32-37.

Illustration 3-3a

Rose Anna's
Form 1040A

Front Side

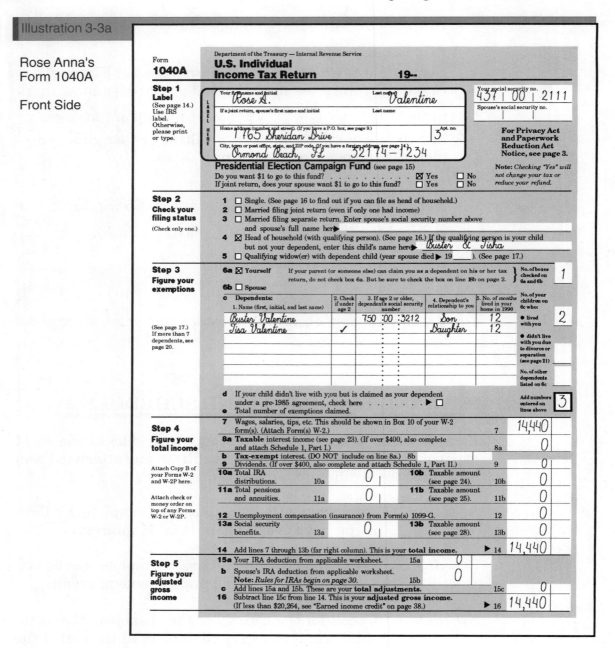

Step 1. Enter your name, address, and social security number. If you are filing jointly, enter your spouse's name, address and social security number. Indicate if you do or do not want $1 to go to the Presidential Election Campaign fund.

Step 2. Indicate your filing status. Your **filing status** is the category in which you file your tax return. In general, your filing status depends on whether you are considered single or married. The filing status that will usually result in paying the highest tax is at the top of the list on page 34. The ones that will usually result in payment of the lowest tax are listed last. If more than one status applies to you, choose the one that will give you the lowest tax. Look in your tax instruction book if you need more information about your filing status. The filing statuses from which to choose are listed at the top of the following page.

Illustration 3-3b

Rose Anna's
Form 1040A

Reverse Side

19--	**Form 1040A**		Page 2

Step 6

17 Enter the amount from line 16. — **17** | 14,440

18a Check { ☐ You were 65 or older   ☐ Blind } Enter number of
if: { ☐ Spouse was 65 or older ☐ Blind } boxes checked . ▶18a ☐

Figure your standard deduction,

b If your pareant (or some else) can claim you as a dependent, check here ▶18b ☐

c If you are married filing separately and your spouse files Form 1040 and itemizes deductions, see page 34 and check here ▶18c ☐

19 Enter your standard deduction. See page 35 for the chart (or worksheet) that applies to you. Be sure to enter your standard deduction here. — **19** | 4,750

exemption amount, and

20 Subtract line 19 from line 17. (If line 19 is more than line 17, enter -0-.) — **20** | 9,690

21 Multiply $2,050 by the total number of exemptions claimed on line 6e. — **21** | 6,150

taxable income

22 Subtract line 21 from line 20. (If line 21 is more than line 20, enter -0-.) This is your **taxable income.** ▶ **22** | 3,540

Step 7
Figure your tax, credits, and payments

23 Find the tax on the amount on line 22. Check if from:
☑ Tax Table (pages 49-54) or   ☐ Form 8615 (see page 36) — **23** | 529

24a Credit for child and dependent care expenses. Complete and attach Schedule 2.   **24a** | 144

b Credit for the elerly or the disabled. Complete and attach Schedule 3.   **24b** | 0

If you want IRS to figure your tax, see the instructions for line 22 on page 36.

c Add lines 24a and 24b. These are your **total credits.** — **24c** | 144

25 Subtract line 24c from line 23. (If line 24c is more than line 23, enter -0-.) — **25** | 385

26 Advance earned income credit payments from Form W-2. — **26** | 0

27 Add lines 25 and 26. This is your **total tax.** ▶ **27** | 385

28a Total Federal income tax withheld. (If any is from Form(s) 1099, check here ▶ ☐ .)   **28a** | 104

b 1990 estimated tax payments and amount applied from 1989 return.   **28b** | 0

c Earned income credit. See page 38 to find out if you can take this credit   **28c** | 583

d Add lines 28a, 28b, and 28c. These are your **total payments.** ▶ **28d** | 687

Step 8
Figure your refund or amount you owe

29 If line 28d is more than line 27, subtract line 27 from line 28d. This is the amount you **overpaid.** — **29** | 302

Attach check or money order on top of Form(s) W-2, etc. on page 1.

30 Amount of line 29 you want **refunded to you.** — **30** | 302

31 Amount of line 29 you want applied to your **1991 estimated tax.**   **31** | 0

32 If line 27 is more than line 28d, subtract line 28d from line 27. This is the **amount you owe.** Attach check or money order for full amount payable to "Internal Revenue Service." Write your name, address, social security number, daytime phone number, and "1990 Form 1040A" on it. — **32** |

33 Estimated tax penalty (see page 42).   **33** |

Step 9
Sign your return

Under penalties of perjury, I declare that I have examined this return and accompanying schedules and statements, and to the best of my knowledge and belief, they are true, correct, and complete. Declaration of preparer (other than the taxpayer) is based on all information of which the preparer has any knowledge.

Keep a copy of this return for your records.

Your signature *Rose A. Valentine*	Date 4/5/--	Your occupation *Clerk*
Spouse's signature (if joint return, BOTH must sign)	Date	Spouse's occupation

Paid preparer's use only

Preparer's signature		Date	Check if self-employed ☐	Preparer's social security no.
Firm's name (or yours if self-employed) and address. ▶			E.I. No.	
			ZIP code	

*U.S. Government Printing Office: 19-- -- 265-058

● Married filing a separate return.
● Single.
● Head of household.
● Married filing a joint return or qualifying widow(er) with dependent child.

Step 3. Figure your exemptions. An *exemption* is an allowance a taxpayer claims for each dependent. List yourself and your spouse if you are filing jointly. List all children of whom you have custody. **Custody** is the act or right of guarding another person. Check the instruction booklet to make sure you have claimed all exemptions correctly.

Step 4. Figure your total income. On line 7, enter your total wages, salaries, and tips. This amount should be shown in Box 10 of your Form W-2. If you have other income as outlined in lines 8 through 13 on Form 1040A, be sure to include those totals, too. Add all of the lines in the Step 4 block. Write the total on line 14. This is your *total income*.

Step 5. This block applies only if you have an IRA. An IRA, or Individual Retirement Account, is for those who do not have a pension plan with an employer, or earn below the level set by the government. Leave line 15 blank unless you have an IRA. Subtract line 15 from line 14 to get your *adjusted gross income*.

Step 6. Enter the amount from line 16 on line 17. Look up the chart to find your standard deduction.

Rose Anna's filing status is *Head of Household*. Rose Anna qualifies as Head of Household because she provides more than half the cost of keeping up a home for Buster and Tisha. The chart showing Rose Anna's standard deduction is shown in Illustration 3-4.

Enter your standard deduction on line 19. Subtract the amount on line 19 from line 17.

Look back to Step 3 on the first page of the form. Find the total number of exemptions you claimed on line 6e. Multiply this number times the figure given for exemptions to get your total. The figure given for exemptions will change from year to year. After you multiply that figure times the number of exemptions you claimed, enter the total on line 21.

Illustration 3-4

Standard
Deduction
Chart

Standard Deduction Chart for Most People

DO NOT use this chart if you were 65 or older or blind, OR if someone can claim you as a dependent.

If your filing status is:	enter on Form 1040A, line 19:
Single	$3,250
Married filing a joint return, or qualifying widow(er) with dependent child	$5,450
Married filing a separate return	$2,725
Head of household	$4,750

Subtract line 21 from line 20. Enter the amount you get on line 22. This is your taxable income. Your *taxable income* is the amount on which you pay taxes.

Step 7. Look up your taxable income amount (line 22) in the tax table printed in the instruction book. Rose Anna's taxable income was *$3,540.00*. She looked up her taxable income in the tax table shown here, in Illustration 3-5.

Illustration 3-5

Section of Tax
Table

If Form 1040A, line 22, is—		And you are—			
At least	But less than	Single	Married filing jointly *	Married filing separately	Head of a household
			Your tax is—		
3,000	3,050	454	454	454	454
3,050	3,100	461	461	461	461
3,100	3,150	469	469	469	469
3,150	3,200	476	476	476	476
3,200	3,250	484	484	484	484
3,250	3,300	491	491	491	491
3,300	3,350	499	499	499	499
3,350	3,400	506	506	506	506
3,400	3,450	514	514	514	514
3,450	3,500	521	521	521	521
3,500	3,550	529	529	529	529
3,550	3,600	536	536	536	536

Rose Anna's tax was *$529.00*. She entered this figure on line 23. When you locate your tax in the tax table, enter that figure on line 23 of your form.

Credits: If you have any of the credits listed on line 24a or 24b, you must stop here and complete the appropriate schedule. Then you will know the amount you can deduct.

Rose Anna pays $40 a month to Care-A-Plenty for Buster's after-school child care. This is a qualified expense. Rose Anna also gives her mother $60 a month to keep Tisha. This, however, is to pay for Tisha's food,

diapers, and other expenses. It is not payment for care.
So it is not a qualified expense. Rose Anna's Schedule
2 is shown next, in Illustration 3-6.

Illustration 3-6

**Rose Anna's
Schedule 2
and Directions**

Schedule 2 (Form 1040A)	Department of the Treasury — Internal Revenue Service **Child and Dependent Care Expenses for Form 1040A Filers** 19--			Your social security number 437 : 00 : 2111

Name(s) shown on Form 1040A   *Rose A. Valentine*

- If you are claiming the child and dependent care credit, complete Parts I and II below. But if you received employer-provided dependent care benefits, first complete Part III on the back.
- If you are not claiming the credit but you received employer-provided dependent care benefits, only complete Part I, below, and Part III on the back.

Part I

Persons or organizations who provided the care

You MUST complete this part. (See page 46.)

1	a. Name	b. Address (number, street, city, state, and ZIP code)	c. Identifying number (SSN or EIN)	d. Amount paid (see instructions)
	Care-A-Plenty	*415 N. Ridgewood Ormond Beach, FL 32174-4551*	321 — 74 — 1234	480

(If you need more space, attach schedule.)

2 Add the amounts in column d of line 1 and enter the total. 2

Note: *If you paid cash wages of $50 or more in a calendar quarter to an individual for services performed in your home, you must file an employment tax return. Get* **Form 942** *for details.*

Part II

Credit for child and dependent care expenses

3 Enter the number of qualifying persons who were cared for in 1990. You must have shared the same home with the qualifying person(s). See page 47 for the definition of a qualifying person.)   3   **1**

4 Enter the amount of **qualified** expenses you incurred and actually paid in 1990. See page 47 to find out which expenses qualify. **Caution:** *If you completed Part III on page 2, DO NOT include on this line any excluded benefits shown on line 23.*   4   **480**

5 Enter $2,400 ($4,800 if you paid for the care of two or more qualifying persons).   5   **2,400**

6 If you completed Part III on page 2, enter the **excluded benefits**, if any, from line 23.   6

7 Subtract line 6 from line 5. (If line 6 is equal to or more than line 5, STOP HERE; you cannot claim the credit.)   7   **2,400**

8 Compare the amounts on lines 4 and 7. Enter the **smaller** of the two amounts here.   8   **480**

9 You **must** enter your **earned income.** (See page 48 for the definition of earned income.)   9   **14,400**

10 If you are married filing a joint return, you **must** enter your spouse's earned income. (If spouse was a full-time student or disabled, see the instructions for the amount to enter.)   10

11 If you are married filing a joint return, compare the amounts on line 9 and 10. Enter the smaller of the two amounts here.   11

12 • If you are married filing a joint return, compare the amounts on lines 8 and 11. Enter the **smaller** of the two amounts here.

• All others, compare the amounts on lines 8 and 9. Enter the **smaller** of the two amounts here.   12   **480**

13 Enter the decimal amount from the table below that applies to the amount on Form 1040A, line 17.

If line 17 is:		Decimal amount is:	If line 17 is:		Decimal amount is:
Over—	But not over—		Over—	But not over—	
$0—	10,000	.30	$20,000—	22,000	.34
10,000—	12,000	.29	22,000—	24,000	.23
12,000—	14,000	.28	24,000—	26,000	.22
14,000—	16,000	.27	26,000—	28,000	.21
16,000—	18,000	.26	28,000—		.20
18,000—	20,000	.25			

13   **.30** x

14 Multiply the amount on line 12 by the decimal amount on line 13. Enter the result here and on Form 1040A, line 24a.   14 =   **144**

For Paperwork Reduction Act Notice, see the Form 1040A instructions.   Schedule 2 (Form 1040A) 19--

---

Complete Part 1 by writing in the information required on the person or business paid for child care and the amount paid.

In Part II, the amount shown in line 12 is the amount to claim for child care. Line 13 contains a table with amounts to match your line 17 of Form 1040A. Multiply the decimal amount beside your line 17 amount times the amount on line 12 to determine the percentage of child care that may be deducted. Write that amount on line 24a on Form 1040A.

Rose Anna's credit for child and dependent care expenses was $144.00. She entered $144.000 on line 24a of her Form 1040A. She did not have credits for elderly or disabled. Write the total amount of credits on line 24c.

Subtract line 24c from line 23. Enter this figure on line 25. If you have advance earned income credit payments from your Form W-2, enter that amount on line 26. Add line 25 and line 26. Enter the total on line 27. This is your total tax.

Enter your tax credits on lines 28a, 28b, and 28c. Your tax credits will primarily be your Federal income tax withheld. The amount of Federal tax withheld is shown in Box 9 of your Form W-2. Add your tax credits. Enter the total on line 28d.

Step 8.   Figure your refund or amount you owe.

If line 28d is more than line 27, subtract line 27 from line 28d. This is the amount you overpaid. You can have this amount applied to your taxes for the next year, or you can get a refund. A *refund,* remember, is payment back to you. Enter the amount you want *refunded* on line 30.

If line 27 is more than line 28d, subtract line 28d from line 27. Enter this amount on line 32. This is the amount you owe. Attach a check or money order for this amount with your Form 1040A. Do not send cash. Make the check or money order payable to Internal Revenue Service. Write your name, address, social security number, and daytime phone number on your check or money order. Write the tax year and Form 1040A on your check or money order, too.

Step 9.   Sign your return.

CHECKPOINT 3-2

YOUR GOAL:
Get 4 or more points.

Read carefully the statements below. Each statement is either true or false. Write *T* (true) or *F* (false) by each statement in the space provided. An example is done for you.

_T_   ● Head of household is one filing status.

____   1. The total number of exemptions claimed is listed on Line 6e of the Form 1040A.

____   2. A refund is money you do not get back.

___ 3. Your taxable income is your adjusted gross income minus all deductions and exemptions.

___ 4. An exemption is an allowance a taxpayer claims for each dependent.

___ 5. Income taxes may be paid in cash attached to the Form 1040A when it is mailed.

☞ **Check your work on page 54. Record your score on page 60.**

PREPARING AN EARNED INCOME CREDIT WORKSHEET

Earned Income Credit is a tax credit given to certain workers with low income. Earned income credit is added to the federal income tax withheld from your salary or wages. If the total is more than your total tax due, the excess will be refunded to you.

All of the following conditions must be met to take the earned income credit:

1. You received earned income, such as wages, salaries, and tips.

2. Your earned income and adjusted gross income are each less than the amount set by IRS. In 1990, this amount was $20,264.

3. You have a child who lived with you in the same home in the U.S. for more than half the year. For a foster child, or if your filing status is qualifying widow(er), the child must have lived with you the entire year. Generally, your child must be claimed as your dependent, but there are some special rules. The special rules are listed in the instruction books for Form 1040 and Form 1040A.

4. You do not file Form 2555, Foreign Earned Income.

5. Your filing status is married filing a joint return, qualifying widow(er) with dependent child, or head of household.

You can take earned income credit only on Form 1040 or Form 1040A. The instruction booklets have a worksheet to figure the credit amount. For more information about earned income credit, call the toll-free IRS number, give your name and address, and ask for Publication 596.

To figure your earned income credit, use the worksheet in your tax information book. Rose Anna qualified for earned income credit. She had a credit of $583.00. She entered the $583 credit on line 28c of her Form 1040A. A copy of Rose Anna's earned income credit worksheet is shown in Illustration 3-7.

Illustration 3-7

Rose Anna's
Earned
Income Credit
Worksheet
and Table.

Earned Income Credit Worksheet (keep for your records)

If your filing status is single or married separately, you may not take the credit. Do not complete this worksheet.

1. Enter the amount from Form 1040A, line 7. Include scholarship or fellowship income only if you received a W-2 form for it.

    1. | 14440 |

2. Enter your total nontaxable earned income. If you have an entry on this line, write "NEI" to the left of the line 28c entry space on Form 1040A. Do this even if you cannot take the credit.

    2. | 0 |

3. Add lines 1 and 2. If this amount is $20,264 or more, stop here. You may **not** take the credit.

    3. | 14440 |

4. Enter the amount from Form 1040A, line 17. If this amount is $20,264 or more, stop here. You may **not** take the credit.

    4. | 14440 |

5. If line 4 is **less than $10,750,** use the amount on line 3 to find the credit in the table that begins on page 55. Enter the credit here and on Form 1040A, line 28c.

    5. | |

6. If line 4 is **at least $10,750:**
    a. First, use the amount on line 3 to find the credit in the table that begins on page 55. Enter that amount here.

        6a. | 583 |

    b. Then, use the amount on line 4 to find the credit in the table. Enter that amount here.

        6b. | 583 |

    c. Compare lines **6a** and **6b** above. Enter the **smaller** of the two amounts here. Also enter this amount on Form 1040A, line 28c.

        6c. | 583 |

If line 3 or 4 of the worksheet is—		Your earned income credit is—
At least	But less than	
14,325	14,350	593
14,350	14,375	590
14,375	14,400	588
14,400	14,425	585
14,425	14,450	583
14,450	14,475	580
14,475	14,500	578
14,500	14,525	575
14,525	14,550	573
14,550	14,575	570
14,575	14,600	568
14,600	14,625	565

CHECKPOINT 3-3

YOUR GOAL:
Get 6 or more points.

Use the information at the top of the next page and the Earned Income Credit Table that is on the next page. Complete the Earned Income Credit Worksheet that follows and write the answers in the spaces provided. An example is done for you.

Jason is married and filing jointly. He has one dependent child. The amount on Jason's Form 1040A, line 7, is $16,275.88. Jason has no nontaxable earned income.

The amount on Jason's Form 1040A, line 17, is $14,275.88.

What is Jason's Earned Income Credit? _____.
(line 6c of the worksheet?)

Earned Income Credit Worksheet (keep for your records)	
If your filing status is single or married separately, you may not take the credit. Do not complete this worksheet.	
1. Enter the amount from Form 1040A, line 7. Include scholarship or fellowship income only if you received a W-2 form for it.	**1.**	**16,275.88**
2. Enter your total nontaxable earned income. If you have an entry on this line, write "NEI" to the left of the line 28c entry space on Form 1040A. Do this even if you cannot take the credit.	**2.**	
3. Add lines 1 and 2. If this amount is $20,264 or more, stop here. You may **not** take the credit.	**3.**	
4. Enter the amount from Form 1040A, line 17. If this amount is $20,264 or more, stop here. You may **not** take the credit.	**4.**	
5. If line 4 is **less than $10,750,** use the amount on line 3 to find the credit in the table that begins on page 55. Enter the credit here and on Form 1040A, line 28c.	**5.**	
6. If line 4 is **at least $10,750:**		
a. First, use the amount on line 3 to find the credit in the table taht begins on page 55. Enter that amount here.	**6a.**	
b. Then, use the amount on line 4 to find the credit in the table. Enter that amount here.	**6b.**	
c. Compare lines **6a** and **6b** above. Enter the **smaller** of the two amounts here. Also enter this amount on Form 1040A, line 28c.	**6c.**	

If line 3 or 4 of the worksheet is—		Your earned income credit is—
At least	**But less than**	
14,125	14,150	613
14,150	14,175	610
14,175	14,200	608
14,200	14,225	605
14,225	14,250	603
14,250	14,275	600
14,275	14,300	598
14,300	14,325	595
16,225	16,250	403
16,250	16,275	400
16,275	16,300	398
16,300	16,325	395

☞ *Check your work on page 54. Record your score on page 60.*

WHAT YOU HAVE LEARNED

After studying this unit, you have learned how to:

- Prepare Form 1040EZ.
- Prepare Form 1040A.
- Prepare Schedule 2: Credit for Child and Dependent Care Expenses for Form 1040A Filers.
- Work through an Earned Income Credit Worksheet.

ACTIVITY 3-1   YOUR GOAL: Get 12 or more points.

Complete Form 1040A and Schedule 2 using the following information.

Dennis Wilson is an unmarried head of household whose address is 1678 Scott Avenue, Killeen, TX 76544-3462.

Dennis works for a construction company as a house painter. His social security number is 407-00-8615.

Dennis' total income was $22,950.00; his federal income tax withheld was $1,890.00 as shown on his Form W-2.

Dennis claims one exemption for himself plus two exemptions for his two dependent children: David, age 4, social security number 412-14-1313; and Susan, age 2, social security number 409-72-4141. Both of the children live with Dennis 12 months a year.

Dennis paid $3,000.00 to the Tiny Tots Child Care, at 1450 Woodside Drive, Killeen, TX 76543-6426 for child care. Tiny Tots' EIN number is 75-473762. Dennis is entitled to a credit which is determined by completing Parts I and II, Schedule 2.

Dennis wants $1.00 to go to the Presidential Election Campaign Fund.

The portions of the tax tables and standard deduction table to which you will need to refer are printed below.

Standard Deduction Chart for Most People	
If your filing status is:	**enter on Form 1040A, line 19:**
Single	$3,250
Married filing a joint return, or qualifying widow(er) with dependent child	$5,450
Married filing a separate return	$2,725
Head of household	$4,750

If Form 1040A, line 22, is—		And you are—			
At least	But less than	Single	Married filing jointly *	Married filing separately	Head of a household
			Your tax is—		
12,000					
12,000	12,050	1,804	1,804	1,804	1,804
12,050	12,100	1,811	1,811	1,811	1,811
12,100	12,150	1,819	1,819	1,819	1,819
12,150	12,200	1,826	1,826	1,826	1,826
		1,834	1,834	1,834	1,834
12,200	12,250				
12,250	12,300	1,841	1,841	1,841	1,841
12,300	12,350	1,849	1,849	1,849	1,849
12,350	12,400	1,856	1,856	1,856	1,856
12,400	12,450	1,864	1,864	1,864	1,864
12,450	12,500	1,871	1,871	1,871	1,871
12,500	12,550	1,879	1,879	1,879	1,879
12,550	12,600	1,886	1,886	1,886	1,886

Form
1040A

Department of the Treasury — Internal Revenue Service

U.S. Individual Income Tax Return

19--

Step 1
Label
(See page 14.)
Use IRS label.
Otherwise, please print or type.

L A B E L   H E R E

Your first name and initial	Last name

If a joint return, spouse's first name and initial	Last name

Home address (number and street). (If you have a P.O. box, see page 9.)	Apt. no.

City, town or post office, state, and ZIP code. (If you have a foreign address, see page 14.)

Your social security no.

Spouse's social security no.

For Privacy Act and Paperwork Reduction Act Notice, see page 3.

Note: *Checking "Yes" will not change your tax or reduce your refund.*

Presidential Election Campaign Fund (see page 15)

Do you want $1 to go to this fund? . . . . ☐ Yes   ☐ No

If joint return, does your spouse want $1 to go to this fund?   ☐ Yes   ☐ No

Step 2
Check your filing status
(Check only one.)

1 ☐ Single. (See page 16 to find out if you can file as head of household.)

2 ☐ Married filing joint return (even if only one had income)

3 ☐ Married filing separate return. Enter spouse's social security number above and spouse's full name here ▶

4 ☐ Head of household (with qualifying person). (See page 16.) If the qualifying person is your child but not your dependent, enter this child's name here ▶

5 ☐ Qualifying widow(er) with dependent child (year spouse died ▶ 19____). (See page 17.)

Step 3
Figure your exemptions

(See page 17.)
If more than 7 dependents, see page 20.

6a ☐ Yourself   If your parent (or someone else) can claim you as a dependent on his or her tax return, do not check box 6a. But be sure to check the box on line 18b on page 2.

6b ☐ Spouse

c Dependents: 1. Name (first, initial, and last name)	2. Check if under age 2	3. If age 2 or older, dependent's social security number	4. Dependent's relationship to you	5. No. of months lived in your home in 1990

No. of boxes checked on 6a and 6b

No. of your children on 6c who:
• lived with you
• didn't live with you due to divorce or separation (see page 21)

No. of other dependents listed on 6c

d If your child didn't live with y;ou but is claimed as your dependent under a pre-1985 agreement, check here . . . . ▶ ☐

e Total number of exemptions claimed.

Add numbers entered on lines above

Step 4
Figure your total income

Attach Copy B of your Forms W-2 and W-2P here.

Attach check or money order on top of any Forms W-2 or W-2P.

7 Wages, salaries, tips, etc. This should be shown in Box 10 of your W-2 form(s). (Attach Form(s) W-2.)   **7**

8a **Taxable** interest income (see page 23). (If over $400, also complete and attach Schedule 1, Part I.)   **8a**

b **Tax-exempt** interest. (DO NOT include on line 8a.)   8b

9 Dividends. (If over $400, also complete and attach Schedule 1, Part II.)   **9**

10a Total IRA distributions.   10a | 10b Taxable amount (see page 24).   **10b**

11a Total pensions and annuities.   11a | 11b Taxable amount (see page 25).   **11b**

12 Unemployment compensation (insurance) from Form(s) 1099-G.   **12**

13a Social security benefits.   13a | 13b Taxable amount (see page 28).   **13b**

14 Add lines 7 through 13b (far right column). This is your **total income.** ▶   **14**

Step 5
Figure your adjusted gross income

15a Your IRA deduction from applicable worksheet.   15a

b Spouse's IRA deduction from applicable worksheet.
Note: *Rules for IRAs begin on page 30.*   15b

c Add lines 15a and 15b. These are your **total adjustments.**   **15c**

16 Subtract line 15c from line 14. This is your **adjusted gross income.** (If less than $20,264, see "Earned income credit" on page 38.) ▶   **16**

19--   **Form 1040A**   Page 2

Step 6

17 Enter the amount from line 16.   17

18a Check { ☐ **You** were 65 or older   ☐ Blind } **Enter number of**
        if: { ☐ **Spouse** was 65 or older ☐ Blind } **boxes checked .** ▶18a ☐

Figure your standard deduction,

b If your pareant (or some else) can claim you as a dependent,
       check here   ▶18b ☐

c If you are married filing separately and your spouse files Form
       1040 and itemizes deductions, see page 34 and check here   ▶18c ☐

19 **Enter your standard deduction. See page 35 for the chart (or worksheet)
        that applies to you. Be sure to enter your standard deduction here.**   19

exemption amount, and

20 Subtract line 19 from line 17. (If line 19 is more than line 17, enter -0-,)   20

21 Multiply $2,050 by the total number of exemptions claimed on line 6e.   21

taxable income

22 Subtract line 21 from line 20. (If line 21 is more than line 20, enter -0-.)
        This is your **taxable income.**   ▶ 22

Step 7

Figure your tax, credits, and payments

23 Find the tax on the amount on line 22. Check if from:
        ☐ Tax Table (pages 49-54) or   ☐ Form 8615 (see page 36)   23

24a Credit for child and dependent care expenses.
        Complete and attach Schedule 2.   24a

b Credit for the elerly or the disabled.
       Complete and attach Schedule 3.   24b

c Add lines 24a and 24b. These are your **total credits.**   24c

If you want IRS to figure your tax, see the instructions for line 22 on page 36.

25 Subtract line 24c from line 23. (If line 24c is more than line 23, enter -0-.)   25

26 Advance earned income credit payments from Form W-2.   26

27 Add lines 25 and 26. This is your **total tax.**   ▶ 27

28a Total Federal income tax withheld. (If any is
        from Form(s) 1099, check here ▶ ☐ .)   28a

b 1990 estimated tax payments and amount
       applied from 1989 return.   28b

c Earned income credit. See page 38 to find
       out if you can take this credit   28c.

d Add lines 28a, 28b, and 28c. These are your **total payments.**   ▶ 28d

Step 8

Figure your refund or amount you owe

29 If line 28d is more than line 27, subtract line 27 from line 28d.
        This is the amount you **overpaid.**   29

30 Amount of line 29 you want **refunded to you.**   30

31 Amount of line 29 you want applied to your
        1991 estimated tax.   31

Attach check or money order on top of Form(s) W-2, etc. on page 1.

32 If line 27 is more than line 28d, subtract line 28d from line 27. This is the
        amount you owe. Attach check or money order for full amount payable to
        "Internal Revenue Service." Write your name, address, social security
        number, daytime phone number, and "1990 Form 1040A" on it.   32

33 Estimated tax penalty (see page 42).   33

Step 9

Sign your return

Under penalties of perjury, I declare that I have examined this return and accompanying schedules and statements, and to the best of my knowledge and belief, they are true, correct, and complete. Declaration of preparer (other than the taxpayer) is based on all information of which the preparer has any knowledge.

Keep a copy of this return for your records.

| ▶ Your signature | Date | Your occupation |
| ▶ Spouse's signature (if joint return, BOTH must sign) | Date | Spouse's occupation |

Paid preparer's use only

Preparer's signature ▶	Date	Check if self-employed ☐	Preparer's social security no.
Firm's name (or yours if self-employed) and address. ▶		E.I. No.	
		ZIP code	

*U.S. Government Printing Office: 19-- — 265-058

Schedule 2
(Form 1040A)

Department of the Treasury — Internal Revenue Service
Child and Dependent Care
Expenses for Form 1040A Filers   19--

Name(s) shown on Form 1040A   Your social security number

- If you are claiming the child and dependent care credit, complete Parts I and II below. But if you received employer-provided dependent care benefits, first complete Part III on the back.
- If you are not claiming the credit but you received employer-provided dependent care benefits, only complete Part I, below, and Part III on the back.

Part I

Persons or organizations who provided the care

You MUST complete this part. (See page 46.)

1

a. Name	b. Address (number, street, city, state, and ZIP code)	c. Identifying number (SSN or EIN)	d. Amount paid (see instructions)

(If you need more space, attach schedule.)

2 Add the amounts in column d of line 1 and enter the total.   **2**

Note: *If you paid cash wages of $50 or more in a calendar quarter to an individual for services performed in your home, you must file an employment tax return. Get **Form 942** for details.*

Part II

Credit for child and dependent care expenses

3 Enter the number of qualifying persons who were cared for in 1990. You must have shared the same home with the qualifying person(s). See page 47 for the definition of a qualifying person.)   **3**

4 Enter the amount of **qualified** expenses you incurred and actually paid in 1990. See page 47 to find out which expenses qualify. **Caution:** *If you completed Part III on page 2, DO NOT include on this line any excluded benefits shown on line 23.*   **4**

5 Enter $2,400 ($4,800 if you paid for the care of two or more qualifying persons).   **5**

6 If you completed Part III on page 2, enter the **excluded benefits**, if any, from line 23.   **6**

7 Subtract line 6 from line 5. (If line 6 is equal to or more than line 5, STOP HERE; you cannot claim the credit.)   **7**

8 Compare the amounts on lines 4 and 7. Enter the **smaller** of the two amounts here.   **8**

9 You **must** enter your **earned income.** (See page 48 for the definition of earned income.)   **9**

10 If you are married filing a joint return, you **must** enter your spouse's earned income. (If spouse was a full-time student or disabled, see the instructions for the amount to enter.)   **10**

11 If you are married filing a joint return, compare the amounts on line 9 and 10. Enter the smaller of the two amounts here.   **11**

12 • If you are married filing a joint return, compare the amounts on lines 8 and 11. Enter the **smaller** of the two amounts here.

• All others, compare the amounts on lines 8 and 9. Enter the **smaller** of the two amounts here.   **12**

13 Enter the decimal amount from the table below that applies to the amount on Form 1040A, line 17.

If line 17 is:		Decimal amount is:	If line 17 is:		Decimal amount is:
Over—	But not over—		Over—	But not over—	
$0—	10,000	.30	$20,000—	22,000	.34
10,000—	12,000	.29	22,000—	24,000	.23
12,000—	14,000	.28	24,000—	26,000	.22
14,000—	16,000	.27	26,000—	28,000	.21
16,000—	18,000	.26	28,000—		.20
18,000—	20,000	.25			

13   x

14 Multiply the amount on line 12 by the decimal amount on line 13. Enter the result here and on Form 1040A, line 24a.   **14** =

For Paperwork Reduction Act Notice, see the Form 1040A instructions.   Schedule 2 (Form 1040A) 19--

---

Complete Part 1 by writing in the information required on the person or business paid for child care and the amount paid. In Part II, the amount shown in line 12 is the amount to claim for child care. Line 13 contains a table with amounts to match your line 17 of Form 1040A. Multiply the decimal amount beside your line 17 amount times the amount on line 12 to determine the percentage of child care that may be deducted. Write that amount on line 24a on Form 1040A.

☞ *Check your work on page 55. Record your score on page 60.*

CHECKING WHAT YOU LEARNED

Now you can see how much you have learned about your income taxes. These 20 questions cover the main topics you studied in this book. There is no time limit, so take your time.

After you finish, check your answers. Give yourself 1 point for each correct answer. Record your score on your Personal Progress Record. The evaluation chart will tell you where you may need additional study.

DIRECTIONS: Each statement is either true or false. Write *T* (true) or *F* (false) in the space provided.

_____ 1. An inventory can help provide proof of ownership.

_____ 2. One important reason for keeping good records is for tax purposes.

_____ 3. Current value of an item is the amount originally paid for it.

_____ 4. A warranty protects against normal wear and tear.

_____ 5. Your employer will provide you with a Form W-2 each month.

_____ 6. A Form 1099-INT will show how much money you earned on your savings account.

_____ 7. A receipt is instructions for preparing food.

_____ 8. If April 15 falls on a holiday, your tax return is due on May 15.

_____ 9. You may claim tax credits for child care expense on Form 1040A.

_____ 10. FICA is the same as social security taxes.

_____ 11. If you are married or a head of household, you may not file the Form 1040EZ tax return.

_____ 12. Each exemption adds $50 to your taxable income.

_____ 13. The Form W-2 is furnished by your employer for the year just ended.

_____ 14. The Form W-2 includes information concerning your income.

_____ 15. The Social Security Administration collects income taxes.

_____ 16. The most difficult tax return form is the Form 1040EZ.

_____ 17. If your filing status is "Head of Household," you may file a Form 1040EZ.

_____ 18. A Schedule 1 must be filed by anyone receiving more than $400 in interest income.

_____ 19. The act or right of guarding another person is called *custody*.

_____ 20. If you have not worked for a year, you are eligible for earned income credit.

☞   ***Check your work on page 57. Record your score on page 61.***

GLOSSARY

A

Adjusted gross income. Your total income minus any allowable adjustments.

C

Charity. An organization or fund to help those in need.

Custody. The act or right of guarding another person.

D

Deductions. Amounts subtracted from your gross pay.

Defect. Something wrong with a product.

Dependent. Someone who relies on another for support.

Dispute. A disagreement between you and someone else.

E

Exemption. An allowance a taxpayer claims for each dependent.

F

Filing status. The category in which you file your taxes.

G

Gross pay. The total amount of earnings for a specified period of time such as one month, two weeks or one week.

I

Income. The amount of money paid to you during a period of time.

Income tax. A certain amount of money paid to the government based on the amount of income for that year.

Internal Revenue Service (IRS). The agency responsible for the collection of taxes.

Inventory. A list of items in your possession.

N

Net pay. The amount of take-home pay you receive, after all the deductions are taken out of your gross pay.

Non-employee compensation. Money paid to a worker who is not a regular employee.

P

Proof of ownership. Written verification that an item belongs to you.

R

Receipt. Documentation of payment made.

Refund. Payment back to you.

S

Social Security Administration. A federal agency set up to provide for wage earners when they reach the age of 65 or become unable to work.

T

Taxable income. Your income less exemption allowances, deductions, and tax credits.

Taxes. Monies collected to help pay for services the government provides.

W

Wages. Monies paid for work done.

Warranty. A guarantee of quality given by the seller or manufacturer.

Withhold. To take out, or hold out, money from a paycheck.

INDEX

1. **F**	9. **F**	15. **T**
2. **T**	10. **F**	16. **T**
3. **T**	11. **T**	17. **T**
4. **T**	12. **T**	18. **F**
5. **T**	13. **F**	19. **F**
6. **F**	14. **F**	20. **T**
7. **F**		
8. **T**		

UNIT 1

CHECKPOINT 1-1, page 4

Give yourself 1 point for each correct answer.

1. **bills and receipts**
2. **major purchase**
3. **charity**
4. **work-related expenses**
5. **payment made**
6. **Form 1099-INT**

CHECKPOINT 1-2, page 6

Give yourself 1 point for each correct answer.

1. **T**   4. **T**
2. **F**   5. **F**
3. **F**

CHECKPOINT 1-3, page 10

Give yourself 1 point for each correct answer.

1. **Tax Information: Expense**
2. **Medical bills**
3. **Utilities**
4. **Housing**
5. **Tax Information: Income**

ACTIVITY 1-1, page 12

Give yourself 5 points for setting up your own personal records system. List of files will vary.

ACTIVITY 1-2, page 12

Give yourself 1 point for each complete item listed on your personal property inventory. Items listed will vary.

ACTIVITY 1-3, page 14

Give yourself 1 point for each correct answer. Count each number listed as one answer.

1. **10**   4. **6, 7**
2. **1, 2, 3**   5. **4, 5**
3. **8, 9**

UNIT 2

CHECKPOINT 2-1, page 18

Give yourself 1 point for each correct answer.

1. dependent
2. Social Security Administration
3. wages
4. taxes
5. exemption
6. Internal Revenue Service

CHECKPOINT 2-2, page 20

Give yourself 1 point for each item of information correctly entered.

1 Control number		OMB No. 1545-0008									
2 Employer's name, address, and ZIP code *All-Rite Tool Shop 4764 Industrial Road San Diego, CA 92121-2405*				6 Statutory employee ☐	Deceased ☐	Pension plan ☐	Legal rep. ☐	942 emp. ☐	Subtotal ☐	Deferred compensation ☐	Void ☐
				7 Allocated tips				8 Advanced EIC payment			
				9 Federal income tax withheld *$840.00*				10 Wages, tips, other compensation *$14,560.00*			
3 Employer's identification number		4 Employer's state I.D. number		11 Social security tax withheld *$1,113.84*				12 Social security wages			
5 Employer's social security number 111-22-3333				13 Social security tips				14 Nonqualified plans			
19 Employee's name, address and ZIP code Felix Herrera 499 Hawthorn St. San Diego, CA 92101-6784				15 Dependent care benefits				16 Fringe benefits incl. in Box 10			
				17				18 Other			

CHECKPOINT 2-3, page 23

Give yourself 1 point for each correct answer.

1. **$5,100**
2. **workday**
3. **income and expense**
4. **$10,400**
5. **itemized deductions**
6. **penalties**
7. **Form 1040**

ACTIVITY 2-1, page 25

Give yourself 1 point for each correct answer.

1. **Jason Greenfield**
2. **407-66-8389**
3. **$16,275.88**
4. **$2,174.32**
5. **$1,245.10**
6. **S & S Foundry**

ACTIVITY 2-2, page 26

Give yourself 1 point for each correct answer.

1. **1040EZ**
2. **1040**
3. **none**
4. **1040A**
5. **1040**
6. **none**
7. **1040A**

UNIT 3

CHECKPOINT 3-1, page 30

Give yourself 1 point for each correct answer.

1. **Line 8**
2. **$10,400.00**
3. **Yes**
4. **$1,144.00**
5. **No**
6. **$769.00**

CHECKPOINT 3-2, page 37

Give yourself 1 point for each correct answer.

1. **T**
2. **F**
3. **T**
4. **T**
5. **F**

CHECKPOINT 3-3, page 39

Give yourself 1 point for each box correctly filled in.

Earned Income Credit Worksheet (keep for your records)

If your filing status is single or married separately, you may not take the credit. Do not complete this worksheet.

1.	Enter the amount from Form 1040A, line 7. Include scholarship or fellowship income only if you received a W-2 form for it.	1. *16,275.88*
2.	Enter your total nontaxable earned income. If you have an entry on this line, write "NEI" to the left of the line 28c entry space on Form 1040A. Do this even if you cannot take the credit.	2. *0*
3.	Add lines 1 and 2. If this amount is $20,264 or more, stop here. You may **not** take the credit.	3. *16,275.88*
4.	Enter the amount from Form 1040A, line 17. If this amount is $20,264 or more, stop here. You may **not** take the credit.	4. *14,275.88*
5.	If line 4 is **less than $10,750**, use the amount on line 3 to find the credit in the table that begins on page 55. Enter the credit here and on Form 1040A, line 28c.	5. —
6.	If line 4 is **at least $10,750**:	
	a. First, use the amount on line 3 to find the credit in the table taht begins on page 55. Enter that amount here.	6a. *398.*
	b. Then, use the amount on line 4 to find the credit in the table. Enter that amount here.	6b. *598.*
	c. Compare lines **6a** and **6b** above. Enter the **smaller** of the two amounts here. Also enter this amount on Form 1040A, line 28c.	6c. *398.*

ACTIVITY 3-1. page 42

Give yourself 1 point for the correct answer on each of the following lines of Form 1040A and Schedule 2.

Form 1040A
Line 6e: 3
Line 14: $22,950.
Line 19: $ 4,750.
Line 21: $ 6,150.
Line 22: $12,050.
Line 23: $ 1,811.

Line 27: $ 1,121.
Line 29: $ 769.

Schedule 2

Line 4: $ 3,000.
Line 7: $ 4,800.
Line 8: $ 3,000.
Line 9: $22,950.
Line 13: .23
Line 14: $ 690.

Department of the Treasury — Internal Revenue Service

Form 1040A

U.S. Individual Income Tax Return   19--

Step 1 Label (See page 14.) Use IRS label. Otherwise, please print or type.

Your first name and initial: *Dennis*   Last name: *Wilson*

Your social security no.: 407 | 00 | 8615

If a joint return, spouse's first name and initial   Last name

Spouse's social security no.

Home address (number and street). (If you have a P.O. box, see page 9.)   Apt. no.
89 Northeast 54 Avenue

City, town or post office, state, and ZIP code. (If you have a foreign address, see page 14.)
Fort Lauderdale, FL 33313-3462

For Privacy Act and Paperwork Reduction Act Notice, see page 3.

Presidential Election Campaign Fund (see page 15)

Do you want $1 to go to this fund? . . . . ☑ Yes ☐ No
If joint return, does your spouse want $1 to go to this fund? ☐ Yes ☐ No

Note: Checking "Yes" will not change your tax or reduce your refund.

Step 2 Check your filing status (Check only one.)

1 ☐ Single. (See page 16 to find out if you can file as head of household.)
2 ☐ Married filing joint return (even if only one had income)
3 ☐ Married filing separate return. Enter spouse's social security number above and spouse's full name here ▶
4 ☑ Head of household (with qualifying person). (See page 16.) If the qualifying person is your child but not your dependent, enter this child's name here ▶
5 ☐ Qualifying widow(er) with dependent child (year spouse died ▶ 19____). (See page 17.)

Step 3 Figure your exemptions

(See page 17.) If more than 7 dependents, see page 20.

6a ☑ Yourself   If your parent (or someone else) can claim you as a dependent on his or her tax return, do not check box 6a. But be sure to check the box on line 18b on page 2.

No. of boxes checked on 6a and 6b: **1**

6b ☐ Spouse

c Dependents: 1. Name (first, initial, and last name)	2. Check if under age 2	3. If age 2 or older, dependent's social security number	4. Dependent's relationship to you	5. No. of months lived in your home in 1990
David		412 : 14 : 1313	Son	12
Susan		409 : 72 : 4141	Daughter	12
		: :		
		: :		
		: :		
		: :		
		: :		

No. of your children on 6c who:
● lived with you: **2**
● didn't live with you due to divorce or separation (see page 21)
No. of other dependents listed on 6c

d If your child didn't live with you but is claimed as your dependent under a pre-1985 agreement, check here . . . . ▶ ☐
e Total number of exemptions claimed.

Add numbers entered on lines above: **3**

Step 4 Figure your total income

Attach Copy B of your Forms W-2 and W-2P here.

Attach check or money order on top of any Forms W-2 or W-2P.

7 Wages, salaries, tips, etc. This should be shown in Box 10 of your W-2 form(s). (Attach Form(s) W-2.)	7	*22,950*
8a **Taxable** interest income (see page 23). (If over $400, also complete and attach Schedule 1, Part I.)	8a	*0*
b Tax-exempt interest. (DO NOT include on line 8a.) 8b		
9 Dividends. (If over $400, also complete and attach Schedule 1, Part II.)	9	*0*
10a Total IRA distributions. 10a 10b Taxable amount (see page 24).	10b	*0*
11a Total pensions and annuities. 11a 11b Taxable amount (see page 25).	11b	*0*
12 Unemployment compensation (insurance) from Form(s) 1099-G.	12	*0*
13a Social security benefits. 13a 13b Taxable amount (see page 28).	13b	*0*
14 Add lines 7 through 13b (far right column). This is your **total income**. ▶	14	*22,950*

Step 5 Figure your adjusted gross income

15a Your IRA deduction from applicable worksheet. 15a		*0*
b Spouse's IRA deduction from applicable worksheet. Note: *Rules for IRAs begin on page 30.* 15b		
c Add lines 15a and 15b. These are your **total adjustments**.	15c	*0*
16 Subtract line 15c from line 14. This is your **adjusted gross income**. (If less than $20,264, see "Earned income credit" on page 38.) ▶	16	*22,950*

19--   **Form 1040A**   Page 2

Step 6			

Step 6

17 Enter the amount from line 16.   17   **22,950**

18a Check {You were 65 or older ☐ Blind} Enter number of
if: {Spouse was 65 or older ☐ Blind} boxes checked. ▶18a ☐

Figure your standard deduction,

b If your pareant (or some else) can claim you as a dependent,
check here ▶18b ☐

c If you are married filing separately and your spouse files Form
1040 and itemizes deductions, see page 34 and check here ▶18c ☐

19 Enter your standard deduction. See page 35 for the chart (or worksheet)
that applies to you. Be sure to enter your standard deduction here.   19   **4,750**

exemption amount, and

20 Subtract line 19 from line 17. (If line 19 is more than line 17, enter -0-.)   20   **18,200**

21 Multiply $2,050 by the total number of exemptions claimed on line 6e.   21   **6,150**

taxable income

22 Subtract line 21 from line 20. (If line 21 is more than line 20, enter -0-.)
This is your **taxable income**. ▶ 22   **12,050**

Step 7
Figure your tax, credits, and payments

23 Find the tax on the amount on line 22. Check if from:
☑ Tax Table (pages 49-54) or ☐ Form 8615 (see page 36)   23   **1,811**

24a Credit for child and dependent care expenses.
Complete and attach Schedule 2.   24a   **690**

b Credit for the elerly or the disabled.
Complete and attach Schedule 3.   24b   **0**

c Add lines 24a and 24b. These are your **total credits.**   24c   **690**

If you want IRS to figure your tax, see the instructions for line 22 on page 36.

25 Subtract line 24c from line 23. (If line 24c is more than line 23, enter -0-.)   25   **1,121**

26 Advance earned income credit payments from Form W-2.   26   **0**

27 Add lines 25 and 26. This is your **total tax.** ▶ 27   **1,121**

28a Total Federal income tax withheld. (If any is
from Form(s) 1099, check here ▶ ☐ .)   28a   **1,890**

b 1990 estimated tax payments and amount
applied from 1989 return.   28b   **0**

c Earned income credit. See page 38 to find
out if you can take this credit.   28c   **0**

d Add lines 28a, 28b, and 28c. These are your **total payments.** ▶ 28d   **1,890**

Step 8
Figure your refund or amount you owe

29 If line 28d is more than line 27, subtract line 27 from line 28d.
This is the amount you **overpaid.**   29   **769**

30 Amount of line 29 you want **refunded to you.**   30   **769**

31 Amount of line 29 you want applied to your
1991 estimated tax.   31

Attach check or money order on top of Form(s) W-2, etc. on page 1.

32 If line 27 is more than line 28d, subtract line 28d from line 27. This is the
amount you owe. Attach check or money order for full amount payable to
"Internal Revenue Service." Write your name, address, social security
number, daytime phone number, and "1990 Form 1040A" on it.   32

33 Estimated tax penalty (see page 42).   33

Step 9
Sign your return

Keep a copy of this return for your records.

Under penalties of perjury, I declare that I have examined this return and accompanying schedules and statements, and to the best of my knowledge and belief, they are true, correct, and complete. Declaration of preparer (other than the taxpayer) is based on all information of which the preparer has any knowledge.

Your signature *Dennis Wilson*   Date 3/15/--   Your occupation *House Painter*

Spouse's signature (if joint return, BOTH must sign)   Date   Spouse's occupation

Paid preparer's use only

Preparer's signature ▶   Date   Check if self-employed ☐   Preparer's social security no.

Firm's name (or yours if self-employed) and address. ▶   E.I. No.   ZIP code

*U.S. Government Printing Office: 19-- -- 265-058

Schedule 2
(Form 1040A)

Department of the Treasury — Internal Revenue Service

Child and Dependent
Expenses for Form 1040A Filers   19--

Name(s) shown on Form 1040A

Dennis   Wilson

Your social security number

407 : 00 : 8615

- If you are claiming the child and dependent care credit, complete Parts I and II below. But if you received employer-provided dependent care benefits, first complete Part III on the back.
- If you are not claiming the credit but you received employer-provided dependent care benefits, only complete Part I, below, and Part III on the back.

Part I

Persons or organizations who provided the care

You MUST complete this part. (See page 46.)

1	a. Name	b. Address (number, street, city, state, and ZIP code)	c. Identifying number (SSN or EIN)	d. Amount paid (see instructions)
	Tiny Tots Child Care	*1450 Bay Street* *Ft. Lauderdale, FL 33317-6426*	*75-473762*	*3,000*

(If you need more space, attach schedule.)

2 Add the amounts in column d of line 1 and enter the total.   **2**

Note: *If you paid cash wages of $50 or more in a calendar quarter to an individual for services performed in your home, you must file an employment tax return. Get Form 942 for details.*

Part II

Credit for child and dependent care expenses

3 Enter the number of qualifying persons who were cared for in 1990. You must have shared the same home with the qualifying person(s). See page 47 for the definition of a qualifying person.)   **3**   *2*

4 Enter the amount of **qualified** expenses you incurred and actually paid in 1990. See page 47 to find out which expenses qualify. **Caution:** *If you completed Part III on page 2, DO NOT include on this line any excluded benefits shown on line 23.*   **4**   *3,000*

5 Enter $2,400 ($4,800 if you paid for the care of two or more qualifying persons).   **5**   *4,800*

6 If you completed Part III on page 2, enter the **excluded benefits,** if any, from line 23.   **6**

7 Subtract line 6 from line 5. (If line 6 is equal to or more than line 5, STOP HERE; you cannot claim the credit.)   **7**   *4,800*

8 Compare the amounts on lines 4 and 7. Enter the **smaller** of the two amounts here.   **8**   *3,000*

9 You **must** enter your **earned income.** (See page 48 for the definition of earned income.)   **9**   *22,950*

10 If you are married filing a joint return, you **must** enter your spouse's earned income. (If spouse was a full-time student or disabled, see the instructions for the amount to enter.)   **10**

11 If you are married filing a joint return, compare the amounts on line 9 and 10. Enter the smaller of the two amounts here.   **11**

12 • If you are married filing a joint return, compare the amounts on lines 8 and 11. Enter the **smaller** of the two amounts here.

 • All others, compare the amounts on lines 8 and 9. Enter the **smaller** of the two amounts here.   **12**   *3,000*

13 Enter the decimal amount from the table below that applies to the amount on **Form 1040A, line 17.**

If line 17 is:		Decimal amount is:	If line 17 is:		Decimal amount is:
Over—	But not over—		Over—	But not over—	
$0—	10,000	.30	$20,000—	22,000	.34
10,000—	12,000	.29	22,000—	24,000	.23
12,000—	14,000	.28	24,000—	26,000	.22
14,000—	16,000	.27	26,000—	28,000	.21
16,000—	18,000	.26	28,000—	►	.20
18,000—	20,000	.25			

13   *.23*   x

14 Multiply the amount on line 12 by the decimal amount on line 13. Enter the result here and on Form 1040A, line 24a.   **14** =   *690*

For Paperwork Reduction Act Notice, see the Form 1040A instructions.   Schedule 2 (Form 1040A) 19--

---

✔ **CHECKING WHAT YOU LEARNED**

1. **T**		7. **F**		13. **T**		19. **T**
2. **T**		8. **F**		14. **T**		20. **F**
3. **F**		9. **F**		15. **F**		
4. **T**		10. **T**		16. **F**		
5. **F**		11. **F**		17. **F**		
6. **F**		12. **F**		18. **F**		

PERSONAL PROGRESS RECORD

Name: _____

✔ CHECKING WHAT YOU KNOW

Use the chart below to determine the areas you need to do the most work. In the space provided, write the total number of points you got right for each content area. Then add up the total number of points right to find your final score. Circle those items you answered correcly. As you begin your study, pay close attention to those areas where you missed half or more of the questions.

Content Area	Item Number	Study Pages	Total Points	Number Right
UNIT 1				
Income and Expense Records	1, 2,3 4	1-4	4	
Inventories and Record-Keeping	5, 6, 7	4-11	3	
Unit 2				
Tax Terms and Forms	8, 9, 10, 11 12	15-20	5	
Getting Ready to File Taxes	13, 14, 19	21-23	3	
Unit 3				
Form 1040EZ	15	27-31	1	
Form 1040A and Schedule 2	16, 17, 18	31-37	3	
Earned Income Credit Worksheet	20	38-40	1	

Date _____   Total Points: 20   Your Score: [ ]

UNIT 1: Keeping Personal Records

Exercise	Score
Checkpoint 1-1	_____
Checkpoint 1-2	_____
Checkpoint 1-3	_____
Activity 1-1	_____
Activity 1-2	_____
Activity 1-3	_____
Total	_____

HOW ARE YOU DOING?

36 or better	Excellent
31-35	Good
26-30	Fair
Below 26	See Instructor

UNIT 2: Understanding Your Taxes

Exercise	Score
Checkpoint 2-1	_____
Checkpoint 2-2	_____
Checkpoint 2-3	_____
Activity 2-1	_____
Activity 2-2	_____
Total	_____

HOW ARE YOU DOING?

23 or better	Excellent
20-22	Good
17-19	Fair
Less than 17	See Instructor

UNIT 3: Preparing Your Tax Return

Exercise	Score
Checkpoint 3-1	_____
Checkpoint 3-2	_____
Checkpoint 3-3	_____
Activity 3-1	_____
Total	_____

HOW ARE YOU DOING?

26 or better	Excellent
22-25	Good
18-21	Fair
Below 18	See Instructor

Name: _____

✔ CHECKING WHAT YOU LEARNED

Use the chart below to determine the areas you need to do the most review. In the space provided, write the total number of points you got right for each content area. Review those areas where you missed half or more of the questions. Then add up the total number of points right to find your final score.

Content Area	Item Number	Study Pages	Total Points	Number Right
UNIT 1				
Income and Expense Records	2, 7	1-4	2	
Inventories and Record-Keeping	1, 3, 4	4-11	3	
Unit 2				
Tax Terms and Forms	5, 6, 10, 13, 14, 15, 19	15-20	7	
Getting Ready to File Taxes	8, 12	21-23	2	
Unit 3				
Form 1040EZ	11, 16, 17	27-31	3	
Form 1040A and Schedule 2	9, 18	31-37	2	
Earned Income Credit Worksheet	20	38-40	1	

Date _____   Total Points: 20 Your Score: [ ]